Heinemann Library
Chicago, Illinois

Mapping the Planets and Space

Ana Deboo

© 2007 Heinemann Library
a division of Reed Elsevier Inc.
Chicago, Illinois

Customer Service 888-454-2279

Visit our website at www.heinemannlibrary.com

Designed by David Poole and Geoff Ward
Illustrations by International Mapping (www.internationalmapping.com)
Photo research by Alan Gottlieb and Tracy Cummins
Originated by Modern Age
Printed and bound in China by WKT

07 06 05
10 9 8 7 6 5 4 3 2 1

Library of Congress Cataloging-in-Publication Data
Deboo, Ana.
  Mapping the planets and space / Ana Deboo.-- 1st ed.
     p. cm. -- (Map readers)
  Includes bibliographical references and index.
  ISBN 1-4034-6791-9 (hc) -- ISBN 1-4034-6798-6 (pb)
  1. Planets--Maps--Juvenile literature. 2. Solar system--Maps--Juvenile literature. I. Title. II. Series.
  QB605.D43 2007
  523.4--dc22
                              2006003349

13 digit isbn hardback: 978-1-4034-6791-1
13 digit isbn paperback: 978-1-4034-6798-0

Acknowledgments
The author and publisher are grateful to the following for permission to reproduce copyright material: Bettmann/CORBIS p. **8**; courtesy Edmund Scientific p. **12**; General Research Division, New York Public Library, Astor, Lenox and Tilden Foundations pp. **5, 11**; courtesy NASA pp. **4** (JPL-Caltech), **5** (STScl), **9** (STScl; Rover on Mars, JPL-Caltech), **14** (JPL-Caltech), **16** (JPL-Caltech), **17** (JPL-Caltech), **18** (Visible Earth, URL: visibleearth.nasa.gov), **19**, **20** (JPL-Caltech), **21** (JPL-Caltech), **22** (JPL/Space Science Institute), **23** (JPL-Caltech), **24** (JPL-Caltech), **26** (JPL-Caltech), **27** (elliptical galaxy, JPL-Caltech; spiral galaxy, STScl; irregular galaxy, NASA, ESA, and The Hubble Heritage Team (STScl/AURA)), **28** (JPL-Caltech); Photo Researchers, Inc. pp. **6** (Ed Young), **7** (David Nunuk), **10** (Eckhard Slawik), **15** (Mark Garlick), **19** (Eckhard Slawik), **25** (STScl/NASA); SDSS Collaboration p. **13**.

Cover photograph of spiral galaxy reproduced with permission of STScl/NASA.
Compass image reproduced with permission of Silvia Bukovacc/Shutterstock.

Every effort has been made to contact copyright holders of any material reproduced in this book. Any omissions will be rectified in subsequent printings if notice is given to the publishers.

Special thanks to Daniel Block for his help in the production of this book.

Table of Contents

Some words are shown in bold, **like this**. You can find out what they mean by looking in the glossary.

Introduction

The Sun, Moon, and stars have always fascinated people. From the beginning, people have looked up at the sky and wondered, *What are those lights? Why do they move?* But for most of human history, it has been impossible to map the locations of planets because they are so far from us. Very few people have been able to venture more than a few miles from the surface of the Earth—and only under exceptional circumstances. And the planets we know about are not very likely to support human life, even if we could get there.

So how *do* we map space? **Astronomy**, the study of space, helps us answer this question. Early astronomers discovered that we could tell a lot about the planets and stars simply by observing what we see in the sky. They noticed that the stars change position in the sky over the course of a night and season by season. Astronomers also noticed that some stars look brighter than others. We know a lot about the stars and the planets—how close or far they are from us, how hot or cold they are—based on the light they give off. In fact, light has a lot to do with what we know about the planets and stars, as you will read later.

The Sun.

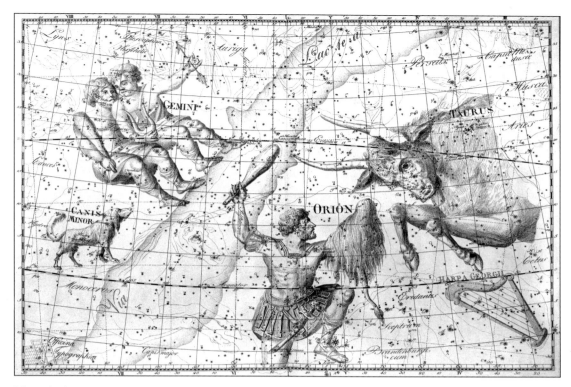

Historical star chart.

This book will introduce you to the tools astronomers use to map space. Some faraway planets have been mapped in detail so that we have maps of their landscape much like the ones made of Earth. Moving beyond *how* we map space, this book will give you information about what we have learned about the planets in our **solar system**. If we ever do visit these faraway places, we will have plenty of maps to help guide us on our journey!

Modern technologies have changed the way we map space. Astronomers can now get detailed images of many far-away objects in space.

A spiral galaxy.

How Do You Map Space?

For centuries, people learned what they could about space by looking up at the sky. They used visible light—the light that we can see—to observe the planets and stars. Using what we know about light, we can gather information about planets and stars, such as how far they are from us and whether they are hot or cold.

Light is a form of energy. The color of light can tell us a lot about its energy level. Think of the light we can see from a candle flame. The flame has different colors—blue at the bottom of the flame, yellowish-red at the top. The blue flame is much hotter than the yellow flame because it is burning closer to the wick and has a higher energy level. The yellow flame is farther from the wick and has a lower energy level, so it is not as hot. In a similar way, we know that a planet giving off blue light is probably very hot, while a planet that has a red glow might be quite cold.

The planets and stars also give off light that we cannot see. As our understanding of the nature of light has grown, the tools we use to explore space have improved.

An astronomer views the night sky through a reflecting telescope.

A telescope is a tool that gathers and focuses light, allowing us to see objects far in the distance. In 1609, an Italian scientist named Galileo first used the telescope to see objects in space. Telescopes had been created for soldiers to use in battle, but Galileo used one to look at the stars. Among other things, he saw the craters on the Moon and discovered that the planet Jupiter has four moons in **orbit** around it.

Since Galileo's breakthrough, most astronomical discoveries have been made using even more powerful telescopes. By the 1660s, the reflecting telescope had been invented. This telescope uses mirrors to gather and focus light. Reflecting telescopes can use very large mirrors to gather a lot of light. This allows them to focus on objects that are very far away.

The next big addition to telescope technology did not happen for more than 100 years. In the early 1930s, scientists discovered that objects in space give off radio waves. Like visible light, radio waves are a form of energy. In 1937, an American astronomer named Grote Reber built the first receiver to collect and record radio waves from objects in space. Radio telescopes are bowl-shaped devices with an antenna in the center. The information they collect is transmitted to a computer that translates it into a picture.

Radio telescopes have added greatly to our knowledge of space because they detect objects that cannot be seen for one reason or another. For example, some objects in space are obscured by dust clouds or simply do not give off or reflect visible light.

Radio telescopes collect data from space that is then transformed into a picture.

In 1961, this rocket boosted the first *Vostok* spaceship and orbited the Earth. The spaceship itself is at the top of the rocket.

More recently, scientists have been able to send telescopes into space. In 1957, the Soviet Union launched *Sputnik 1*, an artificial **satellite**. Less than a year later, the United States launched its own satellite, *Explorer 1*. By 1961, the first human—Russian astronaut Yuri Gagarin—had orbited the Earth in the *Vostok 1* spacecraft.

Whenever astronauts go on a mission, they collect information that helps fill in the maps of space. But people do not have to be aboard a spacecraft to operate telescopes. Many **unmanned** explorations have taken place. On some of these explorations, scientists launch an orbiter—a satellite with scientific equipment on it. Among the most famous of these is the Hubble Space Telescope, which was launched in 1990. It orbits about 375 miles above Earth, where it is outside the planet's **atmosphere**. The atmosphere is filled with gases and particles of dust, dirt, and water—all things that interfere with getting a clear image. The Hubble telescope gets a broad view of space, but some orbiters focus on the planet they are circling. For example, the Mars Global Surveyor has been orbiting Mars and collecting images of it since 1997.

The Hubble Space Telescope in orbit.

Some telescopes mounted on spacecraft collect "flyby" data about the places they pass as the ship heads toward its destination. For example, two **probes**, *Voyager 1* and *Voyager 2*, were launched two weeks apart in 1977. They went on to send back pictures of the planets Jupiter and Saturn. *Voyager 2* continued functioning longer than expected and was able to send images of Uranus and Neptune, too.

Robots in Space

Another great way to collect information about space is to land remotely controlled devices right on the surface to be explored. This cannot always be done, of course. For example, some planets are far too hot and would destroy anything that landed on them. However, there have been successful missions to land exploration vehicles on the Moon, Venus, and Mars.

Mapping the Skies: Star Charts

The oldest kind of astronomical map is the star chart, which shows the position of stars and planets in the sky. Star charts created by the Sumerian people more than 4,000 years ago have been found. Because of the way Earth spins on its **axis**, stars seem to be constantly in motion, moving from east to west across the sky. Knowing their positions was useful in the days before compasses and computers because travelers could use them to figure out direction.

The first stargazers imagined that groups of stars formed pictures, or **constellations**. The names of the constellations hint at their ancient origins. Many are named after mythological figures—Hercules and Pegasus, for example. Others have Latin names, such as Ursa Major, "the big bear," and Sagittarius, "the archer."

Cassiopeia is a constellation named after a queen from Greek mythology.

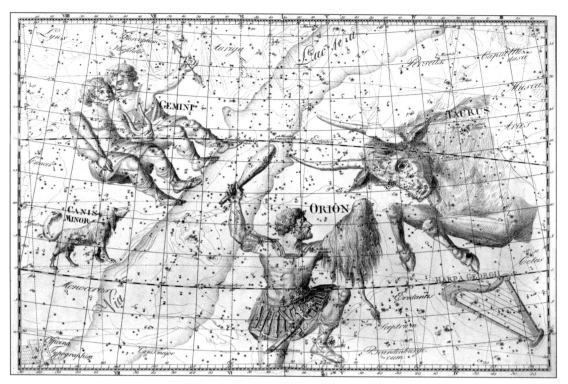

The illustrations on this historical star chart represent the mythic figures the constellations were named after.

Unlike road maps, star charts cannot show distances between objects. All the stars are different distances from Earth, but at night they just look like different-sized twinkling lights against a black dome. This background is called the **celestial sphere**, and it is divided into two parts. The northern sky is the part of the celestial sphere you would see if you were at the North Pole. Likewise, the southern sky is the part of the celestial sphere you would see if you were at the South Pole. Because of the way the Earth rotates, some southern constellations are never visible north of the **equator**, and some northern constellations are never visible south of the equator.

Many historical star charts have beautiful pictures on them to show what the constellations represent. Modern star charts look more like the familiar star-speckled nighttime sky, with labels added. When choosing a star chart, you must take into account where you live, as well as the season and the time you intend to look at the stars. Then you can choose a corresponding map. Because you will need a different map for each season, star charts are often published in collections, or atlases, so that one book contains all the charts you might need. If you look on the Internet, you may even be able to get a star chart for your exact location, the day's date, and the time.

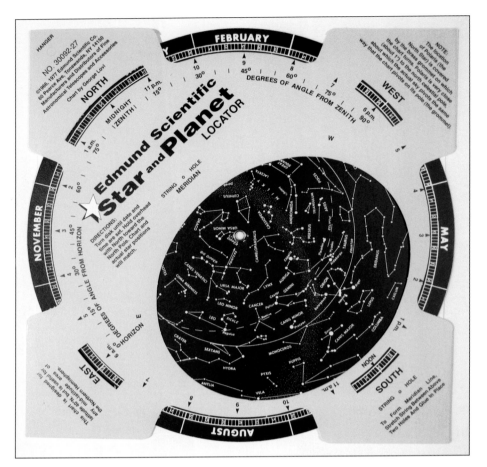

Modern star charts can show you what the sky looks like for a specific date and time.

To use a star chart, first find the **cardinal directions**. When you are outside, hold the map so it corresponds with the direction you are facing (you will want to turn in all four directions to see the whole sky when you use the map). Begin by looking for a major constellation, such as the Big Dipper. Once you locate it, you can search from there for other groupings. A pair of binoculars or a telescope will help you to see even more of the **celestial bodies** on the chart. With practice, you will begin to recognize constellations all on your own!

The star charts used for basic stargazing show only the objects you can see with the unaided eye, or using small binoculars or a telescope. However, astronomers can use special equipment to create much more detailed maps. The Sloan Digital Sky Survey, or SDSS, is a plan in progress for making the most complete, three-dimensional map possible of one-quarter of the sky—the part visible from the Apache Point Observatory in New Mexico. The SDSS telescope is more than eight feet long, and it can spot the farthest celestial bodies known.

Stars are incredibly far away from Earth. To get an idea how far they are, it is helpful to think about one of the units astronomers use for distance. On Earth, we mostly think of distance in terms of miles or kilometers. The object nearest to us in space, the Moon, is only about 239,000 miles away— relatively close! If there were a highway to the Moon and you drove 60 miles per hour on it for 24 hours a day, the trip would only take about five-and-a-half months.

But the stars are much, much farther. Proxima Centauri, the second-closest star to Earth (the Sun is the closest), is almost 25 trillion miles away. That is a huge number: one trillion is a one with *twelve* zeroes after it. So scientists have devised a shorter way to express the same idea: **light-years**. A light-year is the distance a beam of light would travel in a year under very good conditions. This equals 5.88 trillion miles. Proxima Centauri is 4.22 light-years from Earth. Objects in space called quasars are believed to be up to 13 billion light-years away!

This image of the constellation Orion was taken by the SDSS telescope.

The Sun and Our Solar System

Long ago, astronomers noticed that while most lights in the sky stay fixed in constellations as they move, a few follow solitary paths. These are called planets, from the Greek word for "wanderer." Planets do not give off light, though they may seem to. They reflect light from nearby stars. And while stars are glowing clusters of gases, many planets—like Earth—are solid.

Early astronomers struggled to explain the paths of celestial bodies. Ptolemy suggested that Earth was at the center of the **universe** with stars and planets revolving around it. In the 1500s, Polish astronomer Nicolaus Copernicus argued that Earth and the planets **revolved** around the Sun. In 1609, a Danish astronomer named Johannes Kepler improved this model by explaining the orbital paths of the planets. His laws of planetary motion are still used today.

Astronomers believe that the Sun is about 4.6 billion years old.

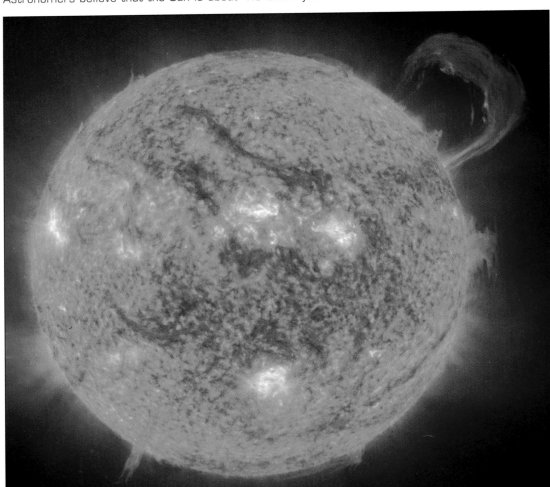

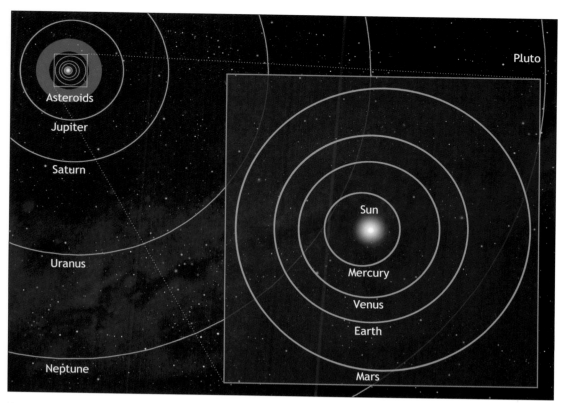

This diagram shows the orbital paths of the planets in our solar system.

The Sun, the planets around it, and other objects held in the Sun's orbit by its **gravitational pull** are known as the solar system. The nine planets we know about, from closest to farthest from the Sun, are Mercury, Venus, Earth, Mars, Jupiter, Saturn, Uranus, Neptune, and Pluto. All circle around the Sun's equator, except for mysterious, far-off Pluto, which orbits at an angle to the others.

The Sun may dominate our sky, but it is a star. It is just so close that instead of shimmering in the distance, it heats our planet, lights up the day, and reflects light off the Moon and other planets at night. It is incredibly hot— nearly 10,000 degrees Fahrenheit at its surface and more than 25 million degrees at its core. And it is huge—about 860,000 miles in **diameter**.

Astronomers have learned a lot about the Sun using telescopes. For example, we now know that the Sun has sunspots (cooler patches on the Sun's surface) and prominences (streamers of gas that loop out from the Sun). We also know that as the Sun revolves, the gas at its center moves faster than the gas near the poles. Various space missions have contributed to our knowledge. The Ulysses probe, launched in 1990, has orbited the Sun twice so far to gather data.

Mercury and Venus

Mercury, the rocky planet closest to the Sun, is the second smallest planet in the solar system. It is named after the speedy Roman messenger god because it moves faster around the Sun than any other planet. Mercury has almost no atmosphere—gas layers that surround some celestial bodies and hold heat near the surface. This means that the side of Mercury facing the Sun is blazing hot, while the other side is bitter cold. An atmosphere around a planet also keeps some objects from crashing into the planet. Mercury has very little atmosphere, and it is rough and cratered because so many **asteroids** have hit it. The largest of the craters, the Caloris Basin, is 800 miles across.

Early astronomers tried to map Mercury, but they could not get an accurate picture through telescopes. In 1974 and 1975, the unmanned spacecraft Mariner 10 swept past the planet three times. The resulting photographs allowed scientists to map half the planet. The other half of the map was filled in using **radar** scans. Another craft, Messenger, was launched in 2004. It is scheduled to carry out three flyby passes of Mercury in 2008 and 2009 and then begin orbiting the planet in 2011.

Mercury looks similar to the Moon because it has many craters. These mark where asteroids have hit the planet.

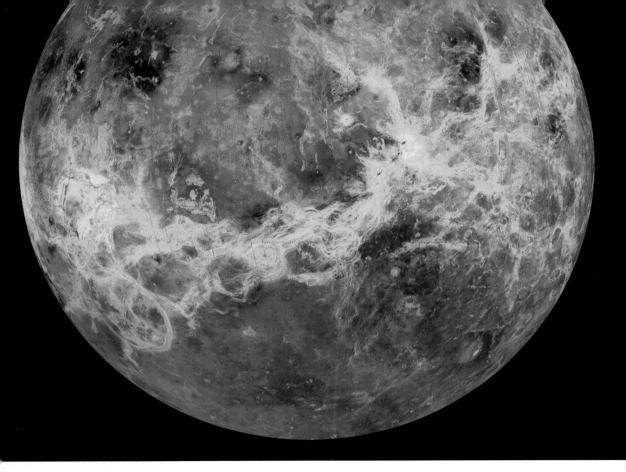

Because Venus is the closest planet to Earth, it shows up brightly in our nighttime sky. Sometimes you can even spot it during the day.

Venus is about the size of Earth—7,520 miles in diameter, compared to Earth's 7,926. It is surrounded by thick clouds of sulphuric acid, so not much was known about it until 20th-century technology allowed scientists to learn more. In 1961, radar was first used to scan its surface. Between 1966 and 1983, the former Soviet Union sent the Venera series of probes to the planet. Several of the probes actually landed on Venus and sent back pictures. Another craft, Magellan, orbited Venus from 1990 to 1994 and used radar to map 98% of its surface.

We now know that Venus is the hottest planet in the solar system—close to 900 degrees Fahrenheit on the surface! Even though Mercury is closer to the Sun, Venus is hotter because its atmosphere is rich in carbon dioxide, a type of gas that absorbs heat from the Sun. Venus is completely dry because water cannot exist in such heat. Even familiar features like mountains and valleys look different there than on Earth, where water has shaped the landscape. Venus also has a few landforms we do not have on Earth, such as coronae (literally "crowns"), ring-shaped patterns of ridges and faults in the ground.

Earth and the Moon

Here on the third planet from the Sun, we are lucky. The Earth is the perfect distance to be pleasantly warmed—not burnt to a crisp—by the Sun's great heat. Our planet has an atmosphere to help protect it. And the chemicals that dominate here, such as hydrogen, oxygen, and nitrogen, help to encourage a great variety of plants and animals to thrive. No other planet is known to support life.

Earth is by far the most thoroughly mapped place in the universe. People have been exploring and documenting the land and seas for thousands of years, improving and refining their maps every time they have entered new territory or developed more sophisticated mapping technology. Even the ocean floor, long a mystery because it is difficult to explore so far underwater, can be mapped using radar.

Scientists used a collection of satellite-based observations to create this image of Earth.

This diagram shows the phases of the Moon.

Early astronomers paid a great deal of attention to the Moon, Earth's **natural satellite**. This was understandable. You can get a good look at the Moon without magnification, and its appearance is fascinating. It changes from a slender crescent to a half-circle, and then it becomes a bright, full disc. Next, you see the other half of the circle, then another crescent facing the opposite direction from where it first appeared. These are known as the Moon's **phases**. They are caused by the Sun lighting up the side of the Moon that faces it. As the Moon circles the Earth, different parts of this lit-up area become visible to us.

The first person to get a clear look at the Moon was Galileo in 1609. Through his telescope, he saw craters, mountains, and valleys. There were limits to what early astronomers could learn, though. Dark spots on the Moon looked like water, so they called them *maria*, or "seas." We now know there is no free-flowing water on the Moon's surface. More importantly, you cannot see the entire Moon from Earth. Because of the way the Moon spins on its axis, only one side ever faces us. Nothing was known about the Moon's "dark side" until 1959, when it was photographed by the Soviet Union's unmanned spacecraft, Luna 3.

Lunar Landings

In 1969, the Moon became the first and only celestial body ever to be visited by human beings. The lunar landings and other space missions have given us a complete picture of the Moon's surface.

Mars and Jupiter

Rocky red Mars is about half Earth's size. It has long captured people's imagination as a place that might support life. This is partly because it has a lot in common with Earth: its day is also 24 hours long, and it has weather patterns and changing seasons. It looks as if water once flowed there (all that remains is ice at Mars's north pole). In the past, astronomers using telescopes observed patterns of straight, dark lines on the planet. Some thought these could be canals built by intelligent beings.

In this image of Mars, the bluish-white areas mark water-ice clouds hanging above the planet's volcanoes.

Explorations of Mars have not found convincing evidence of life, but interesting things have been discovered. For example, Mars is the site of the tallest known volcano in the solar system, the nearly 15-mile-high Olympus Mons. There have been numerous missions to Mars since the 1960s. Sojourner, the first of several roving vehicles to land there, arrived in 1997 and delighted scientists by operating for 83 days, almost 12 times longer than planned! That same year, the Mars Global Surveyor orbiter began circling the planet. It continues to send back data.

Jupiter's Great Red Spot can be seen clearly here. It is the red swirl at the bottom center of the image.

Jupiter is named for the leader of the Roman gods, which is appropriate for the biggest planet in the solar system. Jupiter has more than 60 known moons, four of which are large enough for Galileo to have spotted them. Unlike the planets closer to the Sun, Jupiter is not a rocky solid. It is mostly made up of hydrogen and helium gases. This means that what you see when you look at it are layers of variously colored clouds swirling around in the planet's stormy atmosphere. There are no traditional features, like mountains, to be mapped. However, there is a constant landmark on Jupiter: a gigantic storm called the Great Red Spot. It is a pinkish, spiraling cloud that has been visible to astronomers for more than 300 years.

Scientists have collected information about Jupiter from several flyby missions. The Galileo probe began orbiting the planet in 1995, following a six-year journey through space. It operated until 2003, when it was directed to plunge itself into Jupiter's atmosphere to keep it from contaminating one of Jupiter's moons.

Saturn and Uranus

Saturn, the sixth planet from the Sun, is the second largest planet in the solar system. It is one of the **gas giants**, planets made primarily of gas rather than solid matter. Saturn is famous for its gold and yellow rings. Galileo glimpsed them through his telescope but could not tell what they were. Within a few decades, though, telescopes were more powerful. A Dutch astronomer, Christiaan Huygens, was able to see a single ring in 1655, as well as Saturn's moon, Titan. In 1980 and 1981, the *Voyager 1* and *2* space probes flew past Saturn. The photographs they transmitted to Earth revealed that the planet was encircled by thousands of rings made out of ice and ice-covered particles. Some were bands only a fraction of an inch wide; some were several feet across.

Saturn has more than 30 natural satellites, and Titan is the largest. It is even bigger than Mercury. Titan is the only moon in the solar system known to have an atmosphere. In 2004, NASA's Cassini spacecraft entered Saturn's orbit, then landed the *Huygens* probe on Titan's surface the following year. Scientists expect to gather information from this mission until at least 2008.

This image of Saturn was taken by the Cassini spacecraft.

Uranus, also a gas giant, is the farthest planet in the solar system that is visible to the unaided eye. Until 1781, it was thought to be a star, but then the British scientist Sir William Herschel identified it as a planet.

Uranus appears to be bluish-green because of the way a thin layer of frozen methane gas surrounding the planet reflects the Sun's light. It is unusual in the way it spins on its axis. The other planets all tilt one way or the other, but their north poles point in similar directions. Uranus, on the other hand, is tipped over on its side. Its north pole points away from the Sun.

The best pictures we have of Uranus so far are from NASA's *Voyager 2* flyby in 1986. As the probe passed within 51,000 miles of the planet, it revealed the existence of ten undiscovered moons orbiting the planet. Scientists had already identified five moons.

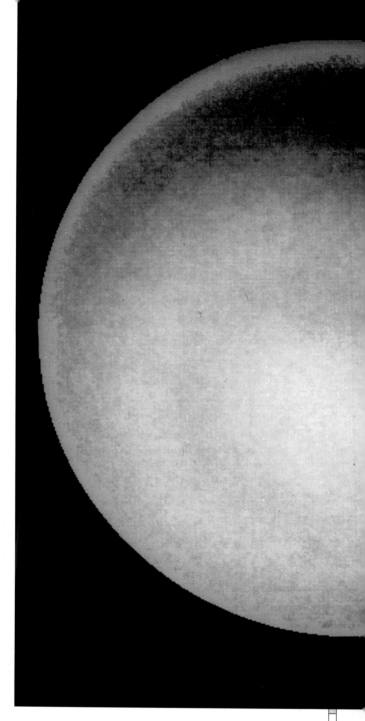

This image of Uranus is a computer enhancement of an image taken by *Voyager 2*.

Planetary Rings

As space observation technology improved, astronomers discovered that the other gas giants have rings. But none have rings as spectacular as Saturn's.

Neptune and Pluto

Astronomers knew Neptune existed before they found it. There were irregularities in Uranus's orbit that could only be caused by another planet's gravitational pull. Working separately, John Couch Adams of England and Urbain-Jean-Joseph Le Verrier of France used math to figure out where the mysterious planet should be. Then, in 1846, a German astronomer named Johann Galle spotted it.

This picture of Neptune, taken by *Voyager 2*, shows the Great Dark Spot, center.

Neptune, another gas giant, is surrounded by methane gas. Like Uranus, it looks blue—but a darker blue, because it is twice as far from the Sun and is therefore lit up half as brightly. It has eight satellites, and one of those, Triton, orbits in the opposite direction from the way Neptune spins. No other large natural satellites are known to do this.

Voyager 2 flew past Neptune from June through October 1989. At the time, it discovered a giant storm, like Jupiter's Great Red Spot. Astronomers named it the Great Dark Spot, and thought it might be a longtime feature. But pictures taken by the Hubble Space Telescope in 1994 showed that it had vanished!

After Neptune's discovery, astronomers still could not explain Uranus's orbit. They decided there had to be another planet involved. The American astronomer Percival Lowell predicted where it should be, and in 1930 Pluto was sighted.

Cold, brown, rocky Pluto has a strange orbit. It is the farthest planet from the Sun *almost* all the time—but for 20 years every two and a half centuries, it crosses Neptune's path and is actually closer. (This last happened between 1979 and 1999.) Also, while the other planets' orbits are pretty much in a line, Pluto follows a path at an angle to the others. Some astronomers think Pluto is not a real planet. They say Pluto might be a gas giant, like its neighbors, and suggest that it is a Kuiper Belt Object, or KBO, instead. That is, they think it is part of a cluster of icy debris at the edge of the solar system.

Pluto is so distant that it has not been visited by a space probe—yet. On January 19, 2006, NASA launched *New Horizons*, the first unmanned mission to Pluto. It is expected to reach the planet in 2015.

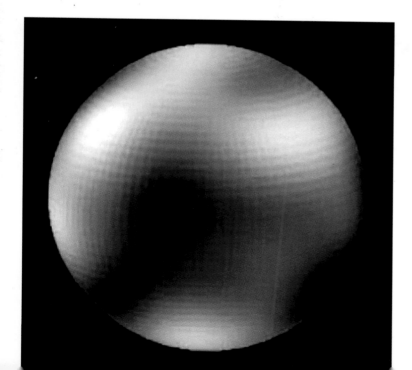

The best information we have about Pluto comes from photos taken by the Hubble Space Telescope.

The Milky Way Galaxy and Beyond

Our solar system is huge—but remember, the Sun is an average star. We now know that there are other solar systems, other stars with their own clusters of planets orbiting them. We also know that stars and other celestial bodies move together, along with clouds of gas and dust, in an even larger kind of cluster called a **galaxy**.

It was difficult to understand the idea of galaxies before the invention of sophisticated astronomical equipment. Before that, astronomers had noticed starlike objects that looked like smudges instead of focused points of light. They called these smudges nebulae, which means "clouds." As telescopes improved, scientists realized that most of those smudges really were clouds of dust or gas. However, a few of them turned out to be faraway collections of stars—galaxies. Three galaxies are visible to the unaided eye: the Andromeda Galaxy in the northern sky, and the Large and Small Magellanic Clouds in the southern sky.

Astronomers believe the Milky Way (shown below) is but one of billions of galaxies in the universe.

And what about the galaxy that we belong to? It is called the **Milky Way** Galaxy, after the glowing band that is visible in the nighttime sky. People named the Milky Way long before they knew what it was. Telescopes helped astronomers see that the glow was caused by countless distant stars. The Milky Way is how the edges of our galaxy look from Earth.

Astronomers have observed many different galaxies outside our own. They have discovered that they come in three basic shapes: elliptical (more or less a flattened oval), spiral (a flattened pinwheel shape), and irregular (uniquely shaped). The Milky Way is a spiral galaxy, and our solar system is located in one of the pinwheel arms. It turns out that galaxies form clusters, too. So we on Earth are in the cluster of our solar system, in the cluster of the Milky Way Galaxy, in a galaxy cluster that astronomers call the Local Group that is part of the universe.

The vastness of space is difficult to imagine. Our galaxy is about 100,000 light-years in diameter—or width. The Local Group is thought to be 10 million light-years in diameter. And then there are galaxy clusters beyond that. It is possible that they go on and on forever. Astronomers have done an amazing job exploring and mapping space, but most of it might always remain a mystery to us.

These images show a spiral galaxy (top), an elliptical galaxy (center), and an irregular galaxy.

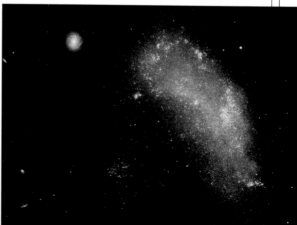

Map Activities

To help you remember the names and order of the planets, make a paper model of the solar system to display on your wall. You will need paper, scissors, and coloring utensils. Because the difference in the sizes of some planets is so extreme and the distances involved are so great, you will not be able to make your model "to scale" (showing the right size and distance relationship of one item to another). For example, if your Sun were the size of a basketball, your picture of the Earth would be no bigger than a peppercorn. Mercury would be smaller than a poppyseed. And to represent the distance to Pluto from the Sun, you would need a wall that was almost a mile long! Instead of trying to make a scale model, cut out the planets relatively bigger and smaller to the others—Earth and Venus should be about the same size and look bigger than Mercury and Pluto, for example. Refer to the appropriate pages in this book to decide how to color them (and don't forget to include Saturn's rings). Then copy the information from the table below onto each planet before attaching it to the wall in the correct order.

Name	Diameter (in miles)	Average Distance from Sun (in miles)	Day (one rotation on axis)	Year (one orbit of Sun)
Mercury	3,032	36 million	59 Earth days	88 Earth days
Venus	7,520	67.2 million	243 Earth days	225 Earth days
Earth	7,926	93 million	23.9 Earth hours	365 Earth days
Mars	4,217	141.6 million	24.6 Earth hours	1.9 Earth years
Jupiter	88,846	483.8 million	9.9 Earth hours	11.9 Earth years
Saturn	74,897	890.8 million	10.7 Earth hours	29.5 Earth years
Uranus	31,763	1,784.9 million	17.2 Earth hours	84.1 Earth years
Neptune	30,775	2,793.1 million	16.1 Earth hours	165 Earth years
Pluto	1,485	3,647.2 million	6.4 Earth days	248 Earth years

Now that you have learned about the planets and space, try some of these activities:

- Have you read any of the myths associated with the gods the planets are named after? Look in your library for a book about the Roman gods and read some of the stories.

- Take a sheet of paper and a flashlight outside one night and make a star chart of the sky (if you live near a city, it may be difficult to see the stars). Try comparing it to a star chart from the Internet that is customized for your location and that date and time. Was your picture pretty accurate?

- Study a constellation chart that also shows the pictures associated with the constellations. Can you see how ancient people imagined those clusters of stars forming those pictures? Pick a constellation and draw the stars on a sheet of paper, then connect the stars with the appropriate picture.

Our solar system.

Glossary

asteroid rocky celestial body that is too small to be considered a planet

astronomy study of outer space, especially the position, motion, and physical properties of celestial bodies. A scientist who studies astronomy is called an astronomer.

atmosphere layer of gases that surrounds some celestial bodies. Atmospheres help trap heat near the surface of a planet or moon, create weather patterns, and burn up some small asteroids or other matter before they hit the surface.

axis imaginary line around which an object, such as Earth, rotates

cardinal direction one of the four main directions including north, south, east, and west

celestial body visible object in the universe, such as the Sun, a moon, or stars

celestial sphere imaginary sphere that encloses the Earth and makes a background for the stars

constellation group of stars in a particular pattern that stargazers recognize

diameter width of a circular object. A diameter is a straight line that runs from one side of a rounded geometric figure to the other, passing through the center of that object.

equator imaginary circle around a celestial body that is the same distance from the poles at every point

galaxy one of the large clusters of stars and associated space debris that are found in the universe

gas giant one of the four planets in the solar system that are made primarily of hydrogen gas rather than solid rock

gravitational pull natural attraction exerted by a planet onto other solid objects near it

light-year distance a beam of light can travel, under ideal conditions, in a year. This equals 5.88 trillion miles.

Milky Way pale, glowing band across the nighttime sky that is caused by the distant stars clustered around the edges of our galaxy

natural satellite celestial body that orbits another, larger celestial body

orbit path of a celestial body around another larger celestial body, such as the Sun

phase differing appearance of a moon (or planet), according to how the Sun is lighting it up at that time. We are most familiar with the Moon's phases. The planets have phases too, but they are not as easy to see from Earth.

probe satellite or other spacecraft designed to explore the solar system and send data back to Earth

radar short for "radio detecting and ranging." A special device that sends out electromagnetic waves. When the waves hit an object, they bounce back to where they started and a receiver translates the information to show the shape of that object.

revolve move in a circular movement, either around an object or on a central axis

satellite object that orbits a planet to send back information

solar system star and the planets that are in orbit around it. Usually the term is applied to our own solar system, which circles the Sun.

universe also called the cosmos. All of space and everything in it, including planets, stars, solar systems, galaxies, and beyond.

unmanned not having any persons aboard

Further Reading

Challoner, Jack. *The Atlas of Space*. Minneapolis: Millbrook Press, Inc., 2001.

Price, Frederick William. *The Planet Observer's Handbook*. New York: Cambridge University Press, 2000.

Ridpath, Ian. *Norton's Star Atlas and Reference Handbook*. New York: Pi Press, 2003.

Wright, Kenneth. *Scholastic Atlas of Space*. New York: Scholastic Reference, 2005.

Index

Italicized numbers indicate illustrations, photographs, or maps.